Vocabulary Test Prep

Cloze • Words in Context • Words With Multiple Meanings

Grades 5 – 8

Written by Linda Schwartz • Illustrated by Bev Armstrong

The Learning Works

Edited by Kate Amerikaner

Typesetting and design by Clark Editorial & Design

Contents

Section 1 ◆ Cloze ◆ 7–26

Section 2 ◆ Words in Context ◆ 27–44

Section 3 ◆ Words With Multiple Meanings ◆ 45–56

Vocabulary Test Prep
© The Learning Works, Inc.

To the teacher
Ask students to underline their word choices on each page (except pages 47-48). Then have them fill in the bubbles on these reproducible answer sheets as you cover each section of this book.

Section 1 Answer Sheet

Student's Name _____

Activity _____

Page Number _____

	a b c d		a b c d
1.	O O O O	8.	O O O O
2.	O O O O	9.	O O O O
3.	O O O O	10.	O O O O
4.	O O O O	11.	O O O O
5.	O O O O	12.	O O O O
6.	O O O O	13.	O O O O
7.	O O O O	14.	O O O O

Section 2 Answer Sheet

Student's Name _____

Activity _____

Page Number _____

	a b c d		a b c d
1.	O O O O	7.	O O O O
2.	O O O O	8.	O O O O
3.	O O O O	9.	O O O O
4.	O O O O	10.	O O O O
5.	O O O O	11.	O O O O
6.	O O O O	12.	O O O O

Section 3 Answer Sheet

Student's Name _____

Activity _____

Page Number _____

	a b c d
1.	O O O O
2.	O O O O
3.	O O O O
4.	O O O O
5.	O O O O

Record Sheet

Student's Name _____

	Page Number(s) of Activity	Number of Possible Answers	Number of Correct Answers	Percent Score
CLOZE	10-11	14		
	12-13	14		
	14-15	14		
	16-17	14		
	18-19	14		
	20-21	14		
	22-23	14		
	24-25	14		
WORDS IN CONTEXT	28-29	12		
	30-31	12		
	32-33	12		
	34-35	12		
	36-37	12		
	38-39	12		
	40-41	12		
	42-43	12		
WORDS WITH MULTIPLE MEANINGS	47	12		
	48	12		
	49	5		
	50	5		
	51	5		
	52	5		
	53	5		
	54	5		
	55	5		

Vocabulary Test Prep
© The Learning Works, Inc.

Percentage Table

Number of Answers Needed	Number of Correct Answers													
	1	2	3	4	5	6	7	8	9	10	11	12	13	14
1	100													
2	50	100												
3	33	67	100											
4	25	50	75	100										
5	20	40	60	80	100									
6	17	33	50	67	83	100								
7	14	29	43	57	71	86	100							
8	13	25	38	50	63	75	88	100						
9	11	22	33	44	56	67	78	89	100					
10	10	20	30	40	50	60	70	80	90	100				
11	9	18	27	36	45	55	64	73	82	91	100			
12	8	17	25	33	42	50	58	67	75	83	92	100		
13	8	15	23	31	38	46	54	62	69	77	85	92	100	
14	7	14	21	29	36	43	50	57	64	71	79	86	93	100

Section 1
Cloze

All About Cloze

What is cloze? **Cloze** is the process of making a connection between two ideas or of completing a thought. When a text passage is prepared in cloze format, some words are purposely left out. Spaces or lines are inserted to indicate where these words have been omitted. You must use the meaning and structure of the remaining text to determine which word could be used to fill each space and restore the proper meaning to the passage.

In standard cloze format, words are omitted in a regular pattern from a passage of text. Typically, every fifth, eighth, or eleventh word is left out. This rigid format is used in cloze materials written for testing purposes. For instructional purposes, the standard cloze format has been modified for the exercises in this book. In the modified format, any word that is syntactically correct and does not alter the meaning of the passage can be accepted as a correct answer.

The practice exercises in *Vocabulary Test Prep* have been designed to help you increase your scores on the comprehension and vocabulary sections of standardized tests. For each numbered blank in the cloze passages, you will be given four possible word choices. However, only one of these word responses is correct. Underline the correct word choice, and fill in the correct bubble on the answer sheet.

Helpful Hints

Here are some helpful hints to follow as you complete the cloze exercises in this section.

1. Begin by reading the entire page so you get an overview of the passage.

2. Notice that words have been left out of the passage and have been replaced by numbered lines.

3. When you have finished reading the entire passage, start supplying the missing word for each numbered line by underlining one of the four lettered choices at the bottom of the page. Sometimes clues to finding the correct word may come in the sentences before or after the numbered line.

4. Reread each paragraph in the passage and substitute your word choices to see if the sentences make sense. If they don't, look back at the words you selected and change the ones that don't seem to fit. Read the entire passage over again for a final check before you turn in your paper to be graded.

- **Noun substitute clues**
  In some of these exercises, nouns have been replaced with pronouns. Here is a partial list of pronouns that can be used in place of nouns:

I	you	it	her	their	that	who
me	she	them	us	none	these	whom
we	he	his	they	this	those	either

- **Transforming word clues**
  Transforming words change or modify the meaning of a sentence or show ways in which things, places, people, or ideas differ. Here are some transforming words that you might find in the cloze exercises:

but	however
nevertheless	therefore
although	whereas

- **Time and sequence word clues**
  Time words are words that tell how often, when, or how many times something will happen. Sequence words indicate the order in which events take place. Here are some time and sequence words to look for in the cloze exercises:

after	finally
before	first
later	second
soon	last
then	next

Vocabulary Test Prep
© The Learning Works, Inc.

Checks and Balances

Directions: *For each numbered line, choose the word that best completes the passage.*
Underline the word you select, and then fill in the corresponding bubble on the answer sheet.

The powers of the United States government are shared by three separate branches. The legislative branch makes the laws, the executive branch enforces the laws, and the judicial branch interprets the laws. In order to __1__ any one government official or group from becoming too powerful, a system of checks and balances was __2__ as part of the Constitution. __3__ branch of the government was given ways to check the power of the other two branches. __4__ provided a guarantee that there would be a balance of power among the three branches.

There are several checks on the president's powers. For example, Congress can remove the president from __5__ if the chief executive is __6__ guilty of misusing his or her power. Another example is the power granted to the Senate in approving presidential __7__ of government officials and federal judges.

1. a. divide
    b. install
    c. assign
    d. prevent

2. a. hidden
    b. established
    c. protected
    d. banned

3. a. Each
    b. None
    c. It
    d. Those

4. a. He
    b. Few
    c. Them
    d. This

5. a. office
    b. voter
    c. officer
    d. checks

6. a. pardoned
    b. therefore
    c. not
    d. found

7. a. seals
    b. appointments
    c. drawings
    d. desks

```
                    C H E C K S
            B
            A       J     E     B
            L       U     X     R
            A       D     E     A
            N       I     C     N
            C       C     U     C
            E       I     T     H
    L E G I S L A T I V E
                    L     V     E
                          E     S
```

Name _____

Checks and Balances
(continued)

The legislative branch of the government also has checks and limits. For example, both the Senate and the House of Representatives must approve a bill __8__ the president can sign it into law. Another example is the president's power to veto a bill passed by Congress. __9__, even though the legislative branch makes the laws, the Supreme Court can __10__ laws and determine whether or not they are constitutional.

There are also important checks on the judicial branch of the government. For example, Congress can impeach and remove federal judges from __11__ for misconduct.

__12__ the years, this system has maintained a __13__ among the three branches of the federal government without one branch becoming too __14__.

8. a. during
   b. after
   c. however
   d. before

9. a. On the other hand
   b. Furthermore
   c. Despite
   d. Since

10. a. review
    b. react
    c. like
    d. hurry

11. a. building
    b. talking
    c. office
    d. writing

12. a. In
    b. About
    c. Over
    d. Under

13. a. court
    b. series
    c. disruption
    d. balance

14. a. powerful
    b. brilliant
    c. expensive
    d. popular

number correct _____

percentage _____

PASS

LAWS

POWER

APPROVE

PRESIDENT

REPRESENTATIVES

SUPREMECOURT

Vocabulary Test Prep
© The Learning Works, Inc.

Congress

Congress is the legislative branch of the United States government. __1__ is comprised of the House of Representatives and the Senate which meet in separate wings of the Capitol Building __2__ in Washington, DC. Elections to Congress take place in November of even-numbered years. People elected to the Senate and the House __3__ to serve their term in Congress in the January after their election.

The primary purpose of Congress is to make laws. During each two-year Congress, senators and representatives introduce thousands of bills. More than 500 bills are passed and signed into __4__ by the president each year. Only Congress has the power to coin money, declare war, approve treaties and presidential appointments, and regulate foreign and interstate trade.

The Senate has one hundred members; two senators __5__ each state. Senators must be at least thirty years old, must have been United States citizens for at least nine years prior to their elections, and must be inhabitants of the state from which they are elected. __6__ serve a six-year term. __7__ one-third of the Senate seats come up for election every two years.

1. a. Them
    b. They
    c. It
    d. Those

2. a. located
    b. recommended
    c. discussed
    d. chosen

3. a. result
    b. depend
    c. require
    d. start

4. a. fines
    b. law
    c. qualifications
    d. companies

5. a. comprise
    b. introduce
    c. elect
    d. represent

6. a. They
    b. Presidents
    c. Them
    d. Congress

7. a. Few
    b. Many
    c. Either
    d. About

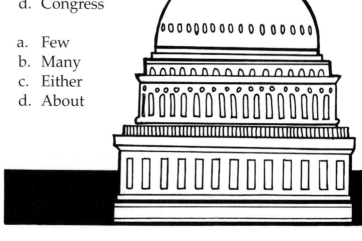

Name _____

Congress
(continued)

One of the responsibilities of the Senate is to approve or reject people the president appoints to high-level positions in the federal __8__. The vice president of the United States serves as the president of the Senate. He or she does not have a vote __9__ it is to break a tie.

The Senate also has the power of impeachment. If a president of the United States is impeached and then brought to trial, the chief justice of the Supreme Court presides __10__ the hearings. Two-thirds of the senators must cast a vote of "guilty" in order to __11__ a president.

The House of Representatives has 435 members, each of whom serve a two-year term in office. __12__ the Senate, the number of representatives from each state is based on the state's population. Each state is guaranteed at least one seat in the House, regardless of its population.

A __13__ of the House must be at least twenty-five years of age, must have been a United States citizen for at least seven years prior to his or her election, and must be an inhabitant of the __14__ from which he or she is elected. The House of Representatives is responsible for legislation that deals with taxes and spending.

8. a. city
    b. government
    c. building
    d. community

9. a. because
    b. unless
    c. however
    d. nevertheless

10. a. under
    b. about
    c. over
    d. with

11. a. decide
    b. find
    c. elect
    d. convict

12. a. Like
    b. By
    c. Through
    d. Unlike

13. a. delegation
    b. committee
    c. member
    d. senator

14. a. college
    b. state
    c. building
    d. home

number correct _____

percentage _____

Name _____

The President

Directions: *For each numbered line, choose the word that best completes the passage.*
Underline the word you select, and then fill in the corresponding bubble on the answer sheet.

The president of the United States is elected to a four-year term in office. __1__ in office, the president lives in the White House in Washington, DC. Presidential elections take place every fourth November. In 1951, the 22nd Amendment to the Constitution was approved; this amendment provided that no person can be elected to the __2__ more than two times. In order to be a __3__ for the presidency, the Constitution states that a person must be a natural-born American citizen, must be at least thirty-five years old, and must have lived in the United States for at least fourteen years.

The president has many __4__ and roles as chief executive. The president heads the executive branch of the government and __5__ the many agencies, commissions, and departments that work to accomplish this job. The president is __6__ for enforcing federal laws, appointing government officials such as ambassadors and Supreme Court __7__, and overseeing the preparation of the federal budget.

1. a. Because
    b. While
    c. So
    d. Before

2. a. military
    b. legislature
    c. presidency
    d. parliament

3. a. commander
    b. job
    c. judge
    d. candidate

4. a. officers
    b. rooms
    c. policies
    d. duties

5. a. oversees
    b. rejects
    c. denies
    d. proclaims

6. a. invested
    b. responsible
    c. stated
    d. seen

7. a. justices
    b. citizens
    c. reporters
    d. assistants

The President
(continued)

As commander-in-chief, the president is the __8__ of the armed forces and may __9__ on them to handle crises that arise at home and abroad. The president can appoint and remove top military commanders. In the role of chief diplomat, the president often __10__ treaties with other countries and acts as the nation's spokesperson in making foreign policy. The president also serves as a legislative __11__ by recommending bills to Congress and working to ensure that they are passed.

The president's salary is fixed by Congress and cannot be raised or lowered __12__ his or her term of office. The president has a fleet of automobiles, helicopters and airplanes to use while in office.

The vice president of the United States is promoted to the presidency if the president dies, resigns, becomes unable to __13__ the duties of the office, or is __14__ from office. If both the president and vice president are unable to serve, the order of succession is as follows: the Speaker of the House, the president *pro tempore* of the Senate, and the secretary of state.

8. a. clerk
   b. governor
   c. judge
   d. head

9. a. appoint
   b. play
   c. call
   d. reinforce

10. a. denounces
    b. reverses
    c. benefits
    d. negotiates

11. a. leader
    b. corporation
    c. senator
    d. follower

12. a. about
    b. above
    c. during
    d. because

13. a. educate
    b. perform
    c. prefer
    d. reform

14. a. removed
    b. settled
    c. decided
    d. resulted

number correct _____

percentage _____

Name _____

The Supreme Court

Directions: *For each numbered line, choose the word that best completes the passage.*
Underline the word you select, and then fill in the corresponding bubble on the answer sheet.

The Supreme Court is the highest court in the United States and is the court of last resort for issues and questions __1__ to federal law. The Supreme Court __2__ as the final authority for cases involving acts of Congress, United States treaties, and the Constitution. The majority of cases it hears come on appeal from the highest state courts or from lower federal courts. The Supreme Court also hears __3__ involving disagreements between states.

The Supreme Court is __4__ of one chief justice and eight associate justices. __5__ judges are appointed by the president of the United States, but must be __6__ by the Senate. Most federal judges remain in office for life; __7__, they are subject to impeachment for abusing the position or for corruption.

1. a. judging
   b. running
   c. voting
   d. pertaining

2. a. seems
   b. acts
   c. opens
   d. looks

3. a. cases
   b. citizens
   c. judges
   d. courts

4. a. heard
   b. comprised
   c. joined
   d. argued

5. a. Them
   b. None
   c. These
   d. That

6. a. counted
   b. closed
   c. confessed
   d. confirmed

7. a. because
   b. during
   c. however
   d. if

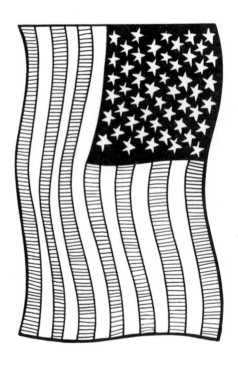

Name _____

The Supreme Court
(continued)

The Supreme Court is in session from the first Monday in October __8__ June or July of the following year. It meets in the Supreme Court Building in Washington, DC.

Each year, the Supreme Court receives thousands of appeals, __9__ it hears only a few hundred cases. Four justices must agree to __10__ a case before it is accepted. Cases are __11__ by a majority vote with a minimum of six justices in attendance. The lower court decision stands if the __12__ ends in a tie. For each case that it hears, the Court writes an opinion — a document stating its final decision and the __13__ for that decision. Supreme Court decisions are important because they help to __14__ the meaning of the laws of the United States.

8. a. after
    b. while
    c. before
    d. until

9. a. but
    b. unless
    c. that
    d. outside

10. a. vote
    b. hear
    c. elect
    d. decline

11. a. witnessed
    b. decided
    c. photographed
    d. convicted

12. a. game
    b. viewing
    c. voting
    d. agreement

13. a. seasons
    b. pages
    c. resorts
    d. reasons

14. a. interpret
    b. injure
    c. enjoy
    d. apprehend

number correct _____

percentage _____

Vocabulary Test Prep
© The Learning Works, Inc.

Name _____

The Declaration of Independence

Directions: *For each numbered line, choose the word that best completes the passage.*
Underline the word you select, and then fill in the corresponding bubble on the answer sheet.

On a spring morning in June, 1776, the Second Continental Congress met in Philadelphia and appointed a __1__ of five men to prepare a proclamation of independence from British rule. The suggestion for this action came from Richard Henry Lee of Virginia. He and other colonists wanted to __2__ all political connections with Great Britain and become __3__ and independent states. Members of the newly-appointed committee included John Adams, Roger Sherman, Benjamin Franklin, Robert Livingston, and Thomas Jefferson. The committee's responsibility was to prepare a document that __4__ with the world the reasons why the colonists were breaking away from Britain. Thomas Jefferson was asked to write the __5__.

On July 2, 1776, the delegates to Congress unanimously agreed to Lee's resolution, and on July 4, 1776, the Declaration of Independence was signed. The colonies __6__ free from British rule and became independent states. The president of the Continental Congress, John Hancock, __7__ fifty-six other men signed the Declaration of Independence.

1. a. member
   b. committee
   c. president
   d. colony

2. a. break
   b. explore
   c. discover
   d. invite

3. a. subordinate
   b. prepared
   c. expensive
   d. free

4. a. divided
   b. shared
   c. assigned
   d. destroyed

5. a. group
   b. colonists
   c. action
   d. document

6. a. concealed
   b. reviewed
   c. became
   d. discussed

7. a. to
   b. for
   c. and
   d. from

The Declaration of Independence
(continued)

The Declaration of Independence contains four main sections. The first __8__ of the document is a *preamble*, or introduction. __9__ states why the Declaration of Independence was written.

The second part describes the principles on which the nation was founded. It states that all men are created equal and that everyone has the same basic rights. __10__ rights are described as "life, liberty, and the pursuit of happiness."

The third part of the Declaration of Independence lists the reasons why the colonists felt they had the __11__ to demand their freedom from British rule. Some of the __12__ against King George III were that he taxed colonists without __13__ consent and that he sent armies to fight the colonists. The king was also accused of keeping British troops in the colonies and hindering the colonists' attempt at self-government.

The __14__ part of the document announced that the colonists were cutting all of their ties to Britain and were becoming an independent nation called the United States of America.

The Declaration of Independence is one of the most important documents in American history, and it has provided the framework for our nation's views on basic human rights.

8. a. part
    b. letter
    c. action
    d. signature

9. a. She
    b. Those
    c. They
    d. It

10. a. Them
    b. These
    c. Whose
    d. Its

11. a. thought
    b. right
    c. might
    d. preamble

12. a. instructions
    b. rules
    c. compliments
    d. complaints

13. a. those
    b. his
    c. their
    d. our

14. a. final
    b. second
    c. beginning
    d. only

number correct _____

percentage _____

Vocabulary Test Prep
© The Learning Works, Inc.

The United States Constitution

Directions: *For each numbered line, choose the word that best completes the passage. Underline the word you select, and then fill in the corresponding bubble on the answer sheet.*

In 1787, delegates from all of the thirteen original states — except Rhode Island — met in Philadelphia to consider changes to the Articles of Confederation. The Articles of Confederation were laws that __1__ the federal government the right to declare war and manage foreign affairs. __2__, the Articles didn't allow the government to regulate trade, raise a militia, or collect taxes. The delegates decided to __3__ a new Constitution, and they chose George Washington to be the presiding officer at the Constitutional Convention.

Some of the delegates wanted a Constitution that gave the federal government considerable power. Other delegates wanted a __4__ central government with more power given to the individual states. Delegates from the smaller states wanted equal representation in Congress, whereas delegates from the larger states felt they were entitled to greater representation in Congress since their states had __5__ people.

The solution to this dispute was the *Great Compromise*, which provided for a *bicameral*, or two-house, legislature. All states, regardless of their __6__, were to receive equal representation in the Senate. Representation in the House was to be based on population, an arrangement that satisfied the __7__ states.

1. a. decided
    b. forgot
    c. gave
    d. installed

2. a. When
    b. Therefore
    c. So
    d. However

3. a. write
    b. expand
    c. open
    d. liberate

4. a. stronger
    b. tougher
    c. harsher
    d. weaker

5. a. fewer
    b. more
    c. smarter
    d. less

6. a. wealth
    b. location
    c. population
    d. climate

7. a. smaller
    b. larger
    c. closer
    d. poorer

The United States Constitution
(continued)

The creators of the Constitution set up a __8__ of government with three primary branches: the executive branch __9__ by the president; a legislature comprised of two separate __10__; and a judiciary, or federal court system.

In order for the __11__ to become law, it had to be approved, or ratified, by nine of the thirteen states. The Constitution of the United States was finally ratified on June 21, 1788. New Hampshire was the ninth state to ratify the document.

In January of 1789, the American people participated in the first __12__ under the Constitution. George Washington was elected president and John Adams was elected as his vice president. The first Congress __13__ in New York City, the nation's first capital, with 22 senators and 59 representatives present.

The Constitution __14__ a framework of government that satisfied opposing views of the people in the 1780s. It has also proved to be a timeless document that guides our government to this day.

8. a. partner
    b. system
    c. record
    d. committee

9. a. raised
    b. footed
    c. headed
    d. devised

10. a. elections
    b. houses
    c. organizations
    d. presidents

11. a. Constitution
    b. medal
    c. vote
    d. view

12. a. session
    b. election
    c. war
    d. meeting

13. a. disbanded
    b. discussed
    c. founded
    d. met

14. a. canceled
    b. vetoed
    c. provided
    d. discarded

number correct _____

percentage _____

Vocabulary Test Prep
© The Learning Works, Inc.

Name _____

The Lincoln Memorial

Directions: *For each numbered line, choose the word that best completes the passage. Underline the word you select, and then fill in the corresponding bubble on the answer sheet.*

The Lincoln Memorial is a magnificent white marble building that __1__ the Parthenon in Greece. It honors Abraham Lincoln, the sixteenth __2__ of the United States. This __3__ is at the end of the National Mall in Washington, D.C. The Lincoln Memorial was designed by Henry Bacon. The cornerstone was __4__ in 1915 and the building was dedicated seven years later.

The building is made of marble and is 80 feet tall. A great hall is surrounded by 36 Doric columns. These columns __5__ the 36 states that were part of the Union at the time that Abraham Lincoln died. The hall of the Lincoln Memorial has three main sections. The center __6__ of the memorial is open in the front. Inside there is a 19-foot-tall sculpture of Lincoln that was __7__ by Daniel Chester French.

1. a. resembles
    b. reminds
    c. replays
    d. retaliates

2. a. senator
    b. president
    c. judge
    d. governor

3. a. window
    b. office
    c. museum
    d. memorial

4. a. passed
    b. harvested
    c. laid
    d. spoken

5. a. surround
    b. investigate
    c. interrupt
    d. represent

6. a. book
    b. section
    c. street
    d. ground

7. a. designed
    b. invented
    c. illustrated
    d. sung

Name _____

The Lincoln Memorial
(continued)

Twenty-eight marble blocks from Georgia were assembled to make the sculpture. On a wall __8__ a seated Lincoln is an inscription that reads, "In this temple, as in the hearts of people for whom he saved the Union, the memory of Abraham Lincoln is enshrined forever."

In the south chamber of the memorial, Lincoln's Gettysburg Address is __9__ in a stone tablet. In the north chamber, Lincoln's Second Inaugural Address is inscribed on a tablet. Paintings that __10__ Lincoln's achievements can be found on the interior walls of the memorial.

The Lincoln Memorial has been the __11__ of many __12__ events. In 1963, Dr. Martin Luther King, Jr. __13__ his famous "I Have a Dream" speech during the march on Washington for __14__ rights.

8. a. above
   b. in
   c. upon
   d. inside

9. a. photographed
   b. etched
   c. televised
   d. knitted

10. a. remind
    b. see
    c. implore
    d. symbolize

11. a. harbor
    b. site
    c. process
    d. statue

12. a. historic
    b. responsible
    c. narrow
    d. approximate

13. a. sang
    b. carried
    c. fought
    d. delivered

14. a. property
    b. civil
    c. housing
    d. court

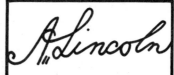

number correct _____

percentage _____

IN THIS TEMPLE, AS IN THE HEARTS OF PEOPLE FOR WHOM HE SAVED THE UNION, THE MEMORY OF ABRAHAM LINCOLN IS ENSHRINED FOREVER.

Vocabulary Test Prep
© The Learning Works, Inc.

The White House

Directions: *For each numbered line, choose the word that best completes the passage.*
Underline the word you select, and then fill in the corresponding bubble on the answer sheet.

The White House has been the official home of the president of the United States since 1800. __1__ contains the president's living quarters as well as the offices in which the president and his or her staff members conduct the official business of the __2__. The White House is __3__ at 1600 Pennsylvania Avenue in Washington, DC.

__4__ the White House was called the President's House, and then, until 1901, it was called the Executive Mansion. That year, President Theodore Roosevelt declared "the White House" to be the official __5__ of the 132-room mansion.

The original building was designed by an architect named James Hoban. __6__ design was selected in a competition sponsored by the federal government. The first __7__ of the White House were President and Mrs. John Adams.

1. a. They
    b. It
    c. He
    d. Those

2. a. universe
    b. county
    c. nation
    d. state

3. a. located
    b. discovered
    c. stood
    d. gathered

4. a. Mainly
    b. Primarily
    c. Possibly
    d. Originally

5. a. president
    b. title
    c. room
    d. building

6. a. He
    b. It
    c. His
    d. They

7. a. occupants
    b. locations
    c. architects
    d. planners

Name _____

The White House
(continued)

__8__ the War of 1812, the White House was burned by British forces while James Madison was president. Later the White House was rebuilt, and over the years, many __9__ have been made to the Executive Mansion. President Franklin Roosevelt added an indoor swimming pool to the enlarged west wing. A second-story balcony was __10__ while Harry S. Truman was president, and the total number of rooms __11__ from 125 to 132.

There are many __12__ rooms in the White House. The State Dining Room can accommodate 140 dinner guests at a time. The main reception room for the president's guests is the Blue Room. James Monroe ordered most of the furniture for this oval drawing room while he was president. The largest room in the White House — the East Room — is used for __13__ guests after formal dinners.

The White House is one of the most popular __14__ attractions in the United States. Each year, more than one million people visit the parts of the executive mansion that are open to the public.

8. a. When
    b. Because
    c. During
    d. Since

9. a. improvements
    b. presidents
    c. architects
    d. rooms

10. a. invented
    b. investigated
    c. organized
    d. added

11. a. decreased
    b. increased
    c. fell from
    d. built

12. a. vacant
    b. casual
    c. developed
    d. interesting

13. a. entertaining
    b. telling
    c. discovering
    d. developing

14. a. government
    b. tourist
    c. senate
    d. garden

number correct _____

percentage _____

Vocabulary Test Prep
© The Learning Works, Inc.

Answers for Cloze Exercises

Pages 10-11 • Checks and Balances

1. d prevent
2. b established
3. a Each
4. d This
5. a office
6. d found
7. b appointments
8. d before
9. b Furthermore
10. a review
11. c office
12. c Over
13. d balance
14. a powerful

Pages 18-19 • The Declaration of Independence

1. b committee
2. a break
3. d free
4. b shared
5. d document
6. c became
7. c and
8. a part
9. d It
10. b These
11. b right
12. d complaints
13. c their
14. a final

Pages 12-13 • Congress

1. c It
2. a located
3. d start
4. b law
5. d represent
6. a They
7. d About
8. b government
9. b unless
10. c over
11. d convict
12. d Unlike
13. c member
14. b state

Pages 20-21 • The United States Constitution

1. c gave
2. d However
3. a write
4. d weaker
5. b more
6. c population
7. b larger
8. b system
9. c headed
10. b houses
11. a Constitution
12. b election
13. d met
14. c provided

Pages 14-15 • The President

1. b While
2. c presidency
3. d candidate
4. d duties
5. a oversees
6. b responsible
7. a justices
8. d head
9. c call
10. d negotiates
11. a leader
12. c during
13. b perform
14. a removed

Pages 22-23 • The Lincoln Memorial

1. a resembles
2. b president
3. d memorial
4. c laid
5. d represent
6. b section
7. a designed
8. a above
9. b etched
10. d symbolize
11. b site
12. a historic
13. d delivered
14. b civil

Pages 16-17 • The Supreme Court

1. d pertaining
2. b acts
3. a cases
4. b comprised
5. c These
6. d confirmed
7. c however
8. d until
9. a but
10. b hear
11. b decided
12. c voting
13. d reasons
14. a interpret

Pages 24-25 • The White House

1. b It
2. c nation
3. a located
4. d Originally
5. b title
6. c His
7. a occupants
8. c During
9. a improvements
10. d added
11. b increased
12. d interesting
13. a entertaining
14. b tourist

Section 2
Words in Context

Name _____

Archaeology

Directions: *Read the entire passage on this page. Twelve words have been printed in bold type, underlined, and numbered. Look at the corresponding numbers and words on the following page. Find and underline the best definition for each word as it is used in the sentence.*

Archaeology is the scientific study of people and things from the past. The place
where the **excavating** work of archaeology is done is called a site. Sites may be   (1)
above ground, underwater, or underground. **Unique** sites have even included   (2)
entire towns that have been submerged due to land shifts. Scientists carefully
map out an area that promises to **reveal** something about the past, and they   (3)
painstakingly measure, dig, sift, photograph, and label what is found. The   (4)
objects can include pottery, tools, buildings, artwork, or bones. Archaeologists
use special tools and equipment to gather evidence accurately and **precisely**.   (5)
The tools can range from huge tractors to small picks or paint brushes. Wire
screens are sometimes used as strainers to retrieve **minute** particles from the   (6)
soil. Finds are bagged or boxed and taken back to laboratories for **analysis**.   (7)

Once at the laboratory, finds are pieced together and studied to determine their
composition. Sometimes tests are performed on them to determine their age.   (8)
Finally, scientists try to interpret all the finds from a **particular** site to explain   (9)
how, where, and when ancient people lived. The archaeologists develop **theories**   (10)
about why people of some cultures gave up hunting for farming or what caused
cities to be destroyed.

An example of an **extraordinary** archaeological find is the one by English   (11)
archaeologist Howard Carter, who discovered the treasure-filled tomb of the
ancient Egyptian king Tutankhamen in 1922. Other finds have even been made
by children, like the discovery of the Lascaux Cave and its prehistoric wall paintings in southwestern France. In 1940, four children came upon this cave while
searching for their lost dog.

Students wishing to **pursue** a career in archaeology usually need a master's or   (12)
doctoral degree. Archaeologists have opportunities to work in museums, in
government service, or as teachers.

Name _____

Archaeology
(continued)

Directions: *Read the entire passage on page 28. Twelve vocabulary words have been printed in bold type, underlined, and numbered. Look at the corresponding numbers and words on this page. Find and underline the best definition for each word as it is used in the sentence. Mark the correct bubble on the answer sheet.*

1. **excavating**
   a. evicting
   b. digging
   c. calling
   d. planting

2. **Unique**
   a. Devastating
   b. Synonymous
   c. Eligible
   d. Unusual

3. **reveal**
   a. return
   b. repeat
   c. record
   d. disclose

4. **painstakingly**
   a. carefully
   b. hurtfully
   c. heartlessly
   d. partially

5. **precisely**
   a. exactly
   b. moderately
   c. falsely
   d. passively

6. **minute**
   a. enormous
   b. thick
   c. basic
   d. tiny

7. **analysis**
   a. perfection
   b. changes
   c. examination
   d. perception

8. **composition**
   a. makeup
   b. writing
   c. score
   d. deposits

9. **particular**
   a. partial
   b. distinctive
   c. participating
   d. complex

10. **theories**
    a. beliefs
    b. problems
    c. themes
    d. plans

11. **extraordinary**
    a. foreign
    b. extraneous
    c. common
    d. remarkable

12. **pursue**
    a. review
    b. purge
    c. deliver
    d. seek

number correct _____

percentage _____

Vocabulary Test Prep
© The Learning Works, Inc.

Name _____

The Architecture and Art of Ancient Egypt

Directions: *Read the entire passage on this page. Twelve words have been printed in bold type, underlined, and numbered. Look at the corresponding numbers and words on the following page. Find and underline the best definition for each word as it is used in the sentence.*

Ancient Egypt was the **site** of one of the world's first civilizations. One of the   (1)
most **renowned** achievements of the ancient Egyptians was the pyramids that   (2)
they built as tombs for their rulers. The most famous pyramids are found in
Giza. In fact, three of these pyramids **rank** as one of the Seven Wonders of the   (3)
Ancient World. These gigantic stone structures have been preserved for more
than 4,500 years. The Great Pyramid at Giza is 450 feet high, and its base covers
more than thirteen acres. More than two million limestone blocks were used in
building this architectural **wonder**.   (4)

The ancient Egyptians were also noted for their limestone temples. Inside
many of these temples was a small **shrine**, an open courtyard, and a large hall   (5)
lined with columns. Sculptors decorated the temples with carvings that
showed **significant** events in daily Egyptian life, such as festivals and military   (6)
victories. They also carved sphinxes that were supposed to guard the temple
and the tombs. These sphinxes represented Egyptian kings and gods. The
Great Sphinx, near the Great Pyramid at Giza, has the head of a human and the
body of a lion. It is **approximately** 66 feet high and 240 feet long. The ancient   (7)
Egyptians considered the cat a **sacred** animal, so many smaller sculptures   (8)
included **images** of cats.   (9)

The ancient Egyptians believed in **reincarnation**. Artists covered the walls of   (10)
tombs with imaginative scenes depicting daily life and **pictorial** guides to the   (11)
afterlife. The owners of the tombs had their likenesses put in the pictures and
believed that the pictures came to life in the next world.

The ancient Egyptians are credited as the inventors of hieroglyphics, a form of
picture writing. They also invented a writing material that was made from the
papyrus plant.

These are just a few of the **numerous** contributions the ancient Egyptians made   (12)
to the development of civilization.

Name _____

The Architecture and Art
of Ancient Egypt
(continued)

Directions: *Read the entire passage on page 30. Twelve vocabulary words have been printed in bold type, underlined, and numbered. Look at the corresponding numbers and words on this page. Find and underline the best definition for each word as it is used in the sentence. Mark the correct bubble on the answer sheet.*

1. **site**
   a. history
   b. home
   c. language
   d. location

2. **renowned**
   a. famous
   b. renovated
   c. heinous
   d. elaborate

3. **rank**
   a. regulate
   b. repeat
   c. transcribe
   d. rate

4. **feat**
   a. feast
   b. achievement
   c. distribution
   d. example

5. **shrine**
   a. kitchen
   b. window ornament
   c. sanctuary
   d. alcove

6. **significant**
   a. tremendous
   b. religious
   c. important
   d. conspicuous

7. **approximately**
   a. precisely
   b. about
   c. carefully
   d. realistically

8. **sacred**
   a. frightened
   b. lonely
   c. holy
   d. scarce

9. **images**
   a. depictions
   b. imaginations
   c. captions
   d. deceptions

10. **reincarnation**
    a. crowning of a king
    b. rebirth
    c. celebration
    d. ritual

11. **pictorial**
    a. photographic
    b. farmlike
    c. gorgeous
    d. graphic

12. **numerous**
    a. many
    b. critical
    c. vital
    d. important

number correct _____

percentage _____

Vocabulary Test Prep
© The Learning Works, Inc.

Name _____

The Aztecs

Directions: Read the entire passage on this page. Twelve words have been printed in bold type, underlined, and numbered. Look at the corresponding numbers and words on the following page. Find and underline the best definition for each word as it is used in the sentence.

The Aztecs were an important group who ruled a **mighty** empire in Mexico dur-   (1)
ing the early 1500s. The Aztecs conquered most of central Mexico and forced
their **captives** to give them gold, cotton, and corn. They built a capital city, called   (2)
Tenochtitlan, where Mexico City now stands.

A council of high-ranking nobles selected an emperor from a royal family to rule
the Aztec empire. **Prior** to making important decisions, the ruling emperor had   (3)
to **consult** with the Council of Nobles. One of the most famous Aztec rulers was   (4)
Montezuma II who ruled from 1502 to 1520.

The Aztecs designed **elaborate** sculptures that **adorned** their temples and build-   (5)(6)
ings. The Aztec Calendar Stone is one of the most famous surviving sculptures.
This large, circular stone measures about twelve feet in diameter. The face of the
Aztec sun god is in the center of the stone. Other ornate carvings **depict** days of   (7)
the month or religious symbols.

The Aztecs used a form of writing **comprised** of pictographs, or small pictures   (8)
that **symbolized** ideas and sounds of syllables. The Aztecs used the pictographs   (9)
for religious writing, for recording historical events, for business **transactions**,   (10)
and for taking censuses.

Aztec homes were simple and **practical**. Homes were made of adobe in the high-   (11)
lands and of reed and clay in the lowlands. Many families also had a storehouse
and a sweathouse — for steam baths — in addition to their main **dwelling**.   (12)

The Aztec empire was destroyed by the Spaniards in 1521, but the Aztec people
left an important mark on Mexican culture.

Name _____

The Aztecs
(continued)

Directions: Read the entire passage on page 32. Twelve vocabulary words
have been printed in bold type, underlined, and numbered. Look at the corresponding
numbers and words on this page. Find and underline the best definition for each word
as it is used in the sentence. Mark the correct bubble on the answer sheet.

1. **mighty**
   a. passive
   b. powerful
   c. model
   d. moralistic

2. **captives**
   a. rulers
   b. leaders
   c. captains
   d. prisoners

3. **Prior**
   a. After
   b. Before
   c. Soon
   d. During

4. **consult**
   a. contain
   b. grant permission
   c. continue
   d. confer

5. **elaborate**
   a. ornate
   b. simple
   c. soft
   d. elementary

6. **adorned**
   a. admired
   b. advertised
   c. decorated
   d. alternated

7. **depict**
   a. displace
   b. despise
   c. represent
   d. transcribe

8. **comprised**
   a. made up
   b. gave up
   c. concealed
   d. chosen

9. **symbolized**
   a. attributed
   b. stated
   c. surrounded
   d. represented

10. **transactions**
    a. discoveries
    b. deals
    c. rules
    d. transcripts

11. **practical**
    a. immaculate
    b. cozy
    c. sensible
    d. pristine

12. **dwelling**
    a. tribe
    b. community
    c. home
    d. occupation

number correct _____

percentage _____

33

Name _____

The Lewis and Clark Expedition

Directions: *Read the entire passage on this page. Twelve words have been printed in bold type, underlined, and numbered. Look at the corresponding numbers and words on the following page. Find and underline the best definition for each word as it is used in the sentence.*

Although the Louisiana Purchase was **hailed** as a tremendous bargain, no one (1)
was exactly certain what the United States had **acquired** from the French in (2)
1803. To answer questions about the acquisition, President Thomas Jefferson
commissioned Meriwether Lewis, his private secretary, to explore the territory. (3)
Lewis chose William Clark as his co-leader.

The goals of the expedition were to search for a practical land-water **route** to the (4)
Pacific Ocean and to explore the uncharted west. The purpose of this route
across the continent was to prepare the way for a commercial exchange with the
Native Americans they met, to open the west for settlement, and to establish a
lucrative fur trade. Meriwether Lewis and William Clark were requested to keep (5)
meticulous records of the climate, mineral resources, wildlife, soil conditions, (6)
and geographical features they observed in the new territory. They were also
instructed by President Jefferson to record tribal **affiliations** and interesting cus- (7)
toms of any Native Americans they **encountered**. (8)

In May of 1804, the Lewis and Clark expedition left St. Louis, Missouri, and traveled northwest along the Missouri River. More than forty frontiersmen and
hunters accompanied Meriwether Lewis and William Clark on the first **leg** of (9)
their journey. Lewis and Clark left with three boats. These vessels were stocked
with food, medical supplies, ammunition, and **trinkets** for trade with the Native (10)
Americans. But when the men reached the Great Falls of the Missouri, their
boats were crushed by the huge rocks and churning rapids.

The men had no contact with home for more than two years, and they faced
many hardships along the way. They encountered obstacles that no one had
anticipated at the **outset**, including the need to row upstream against a much (11)
stiffer current than anyone had anticipated.

In the fall of 1804, the group reached a Mandan Native American village near
present-day Bismarck, North Dakota. There they hired a French-Canadian fur
trader as an interpreter. His wife, Sacajawea, was a Shoshone woman who
offered to guide the expedition across the steep Rocky Mountains.

Lewis and Clark sent reports and maps back to President Jefferson that gave
an insight into the region west of the Mississippi River. Their **arduous** journey (12)
also helped stimulate the fur trade.

Name _____

The Lewis and Clark Expedition

(continued)

Directions: Read the entire passage on page 34. Twelve vocabulary words have been printed in bold type, underlined, and numbered. Look at the corresponding numbers and words on this page. Find and underline the best definition for each word as it is used in the sentence. Mark the correct bubble on the answer sheet.

1. **hailed**
   a. rained
   b. attracted
   c. acclaimed
   d. stormed

2. **acquired**
   a. resisted
   b. declared
   c. assisted
   d. obtained

3. **commissioned**
   a. hired
   b. settled
   c. commenced
   d. deviated

4. **route**
   a. development
   b. line of travel
   c. design
   d. method

5. **lucrative**
   a. probable
   b. promising
   c. profitable
   d. inventive

6. **meticulous**
   a. brief
   b. detailed
   c. slovenly
   d. forceful

7. **affiliations**
   a. leaders
   b. notices
   c. associations
   d. problems

8. **encountered**
   a. met
   b. engaged
   c. decided
   d. rescued

9. **leg**
   a. limb
   b. femur
   c. knee
   d. portion

10. **trinkets**
    a. woolen blankets
    b. small ornaments or gifts
    c. large animals
    d. tents made from hides

11. **outset**
    a. conclusion
    b. beginning
    c. place or location
    d. finale

12. **arduous**
    a. simplistic
    b. everlasting
    c. strenuous
    d. diverse

number correct _____

percentage _____

35

Name _____

Life in Colonial America

Directions: *Read the entire passage on this page. Twelve words have been printed in bold type, underlined, and numbered. Look at the corresponding numbers and words on the following page. Find and underline the best definition for each word as it is used in the sentence.*

In the seventeenth and eighteenth centuries, English colonies in America **prospered** and grew. In the New England colonies, farming was the major economic activity. The farms were unusually small, but the colonists raised a **variety** of crops including peas, corn, and pumpkins. Colonists were also **engaged** in shipbuilding, trading, fishing, and whaling.   (1) (2) (3)

Education was a high priority. Children were taught to read and write so they could study the Bible. In the New England colonies, children read from a hornbook. A hornbook was a wooden paddle attached to parchment with the letters of the alphabet on it. Many colonial children spent years as **apprentices**, learning skills such as carpentry, candle making, or weaving. In 1647, laws were **initiated** that required larger villages to set up schools supported by local taxes.   (4) (5)

The **abundant** forests provided wood for the craftspeople to make their houses, furniture, cabinets, and fences. Each town or village had a blacksmith who used iron ore to **fashion** tools for the home. The blacksmith built farm equipment and used molds to make horseshoes. Men and boys hunted and plowed the land while the women and girls churned butter or made candles and soap. Women in the colonies were **resourceful** and used old bits of cloth and wool to create braided rugs. They also made colorful quilts to **enhance** their homes and make them more comfortable. The quilts usually had pictures of flowers, animals, the alphabet or other favorite scenes. The family's clothing was woven and spun at home.   (6) (7) (8) (9)

The family gathered around the fireplace in the evening because it **provided** light and heat. The brick fireplaces had iron bars across the back with chains and hooks. These hooks held pots over the fire at **various** heights. Fruits, vegetables, and dyed yarn was hung and left to dry beside the fireplace. In a **typical** colonial home, the furniture was simple and might include an oak table around which the family ate, a spinning wheel, ladder-back chairs, and perhaps a wicker cradle.   (10) (11) (12)

Name _____

Life in Colonial America
(continued)

Directions: *Read the entire passage on page 36. Twelve vocabulary words have been printed in bold type, underlined, and numbered. Look at the corresponding numbers and words on this page. Find and underline the best definition for each word as it is used in the sentence. Mark the correct bubble on the answer sheet.*

---

1. **prospered**
   a. deplored
   b. proposed
   c. decreased
   d. thrived

2. **variety**
   a. parcel
   b. growth
   c. diversity
   d. planting

3. **engaged**
   a. married
   b. entangled
   c. involved
   d. transmitted

4. **apprentices**
   a. trainees
   b. teachers
   c. farmers
   d. pilgrims

5. **initiated**
   a. investigated
   b. introduced
   c. copied
   d. imitated

6. **abundant**
   a. absorbed
   b. green
   c. absolute
   d. plentiful

7. **fashion**
   a. clothes
   b. make
   c. dress
   d. style

8. **resourceful**
   a. skillful
   b. respectful
   c. resentful
   d. resolute

9. **enhance**
   a. embrace
   b. engross
   c. paint
   d. improve

10. **provided**
    a. proved
    b. supplied
    c. provoked
    d. purchased

11. **various**
    a. vacant
    b. different
    c. wide
    d. visible

12. **typical**
    a. tasty
    b. tropical
    c. representative
    d. unusual

number correct _____

percentage _____

Vocabulary Test Prep
© The Learning Works, Inc.

Name _____

The Boston Tea Party

Directions: *Read the entire passage on this page. Twelve words have been printed in bold type, underlined, and numbered. Look at the corresponding numbers and words on the following page. Find and underline the best definition for each word as it is used in the sentence.*

The Boston Tea Party was one of the events that led to the American Revolution. In 1773, the British Parliament passed the Tea Act and **granted** the East India   (1)
Company the right to sell tea directly to the American colonies without having
to pay an export tax on the tea. This **enabled** the East India Company to sell the   (2)
tea inexpensively. The Tea Act also helped many members of Parliament who
owned shares in the East India Company. The colonists were not interested in
lower prices. They didn't like the fact that the Parliament could **impose** laws   (3)
that would be partial to British businesses. The British Parliament also imposed
an import tax on tea sold to the colonists, so the colonists **protested** and began a   (4)
boycott of goods coming from Great Britain.   (5)

On December 16, 1773, about fifty colonists disguised themselves as Native
Americans and boarded British ships that arrived in the Boston harbor in
November. The colonists **pitched** more than 300 chests of tea overboard as a way   (6)
of protesting the tax.

The British were **outraged**. In **retaliation**, they closed the port of Boston to all   (7)(8)
trade. Ships were **restricted** from entering or leaving the harbor. Parliament   (9)
declared that the harbor would remain closed until the colonists paid for the tea
that was dumped into the harbor.

Prior to the Boston Tea Party, the colonists had town meetings whenever they
wished. After the Boston Tea Party, Parliament **forbade** the colonists to have   (10)
more than one town meeting a year without the **consent** of the governor. Many   (11)
colonists believed that the British government was infringing on their right to
govern themselves.

The colonists had to **bear** the expense for the British soldiers that were sent to the   (12)
Massachusetts colony. The colonists were required to put the British troops up in
their homes under the new Quartering Act. Because these new laws established
by the British Parliament were so harsh, they were called the Intolerable Acts.

Name _____

The Boston Tea Party
(continued)

Directions: Read the entire passage on page 38. Twelve vocabulary words have been printed in bold type, underlined, and numbered. Look at the corresponding numbers and words on this page. Find and underline the best definition for each word as it is used in the sentence. Mark the correct bubble on the answer sheet.

---

1. **granted**
   a. charged
   b. permitted
   c. increased
   d. deplored

2. **enabled**
   a. rejected
   b. prevented
   c. examined
   d. made possible

3. **impose**
   a. impeach
   b. inactivate
   c. improvise
   d. establish by authority

4. **protested**
   a. provoked
   b. projected
   c. objected
   d. decided

5. **boycott**
   a. refusal to have dealings with
   b. full acceptance of conditions
   c. shortage
   d. concerted effort

6. **pitched**
   a. sloped
   b. through
   c. threw
   d. fixed

7. **outraged**
   a. angered
   b. disappointed
   c. overjoyed
   d. eliminated

8. **retaliation**
   a. restraint
   b. retirement
   c. revenge
   d. resolve

9. **restricted**
   a. repulsed
   b. limited
   c. encouraged
   d. requested

10. **forbade**
    a. demanded
    b. enticed
    c. forced
    d. prohibited

11. **consent**
    a. advice
    b. connection
    c. connotation
    d. approval

12. **bear**
    a. large, heavy mammal
    b. assume or accept
    c. unclothed
    d. allow

number correct _____

percentage _____

Name _____

The Civil War

Directions: Read the entire passage on this page. Twelve words have been printed in bold type, underlined, and numbered. Look at the corresponding numbers and words on the following page. Find and underline the best definition for each word as it is used in the sentence.

In the months following Abraham Lincoln's election to the presidency, eleven Southern states voted to **secede** from the United States. These states formed (1) their own government and called themselves the Confederate States of America, or the Confederacy. Jefferson Davis was chosen to be president. During his inaugural address, Lincoln told the people that no state had the right to secede. He **urged** the Southern states to return to the Union. (2)

The North had several important strengths over the South. It had **superior** (3) industrial and financial strength and a larger population. Most of the railroads were in the North, so leaders were able to send supplies and soldiers to the battlefront more **expeditiously**. The North also had a strong navy and a large (4) **fleet** of private ships. The South had the advantage of fighting on familiar land, (5) and it had excellent military leaders. The Confederate states were also fighting for a cause they believed in strongly — their right to secede from the Union and create their own government.

At first, the South had the upper hand. It fought to protect its territory under the leadership of General Robert E. Lee. The **strategy** of the South was to fight a (6) defensive war. The Union's strategy was to **blockade** many of the southern ports (7) and then attempt to **seize** control of the Mississippi River so the South would be (8) unable to supply its troops.

Gradually, the North turned the tide under the leadership of General Ulysses S. Grant. In September of 1863, Lincoln **issued** the Emancipation Proclamation, (9) freeing all slaves in the Confederacy. In 1865, General Lee surrendered to General Grant at Appomattox Court House in Virginia.

The Civil War had a **staggering** effect on the nation. More than 600,000 (10) Americans died during the four years of fighting. Damage to property was **immense**, and many other Southern towns, cities, and factories were destroyed. (11) The war also caused a **rift** between the people of the North and South. (12)

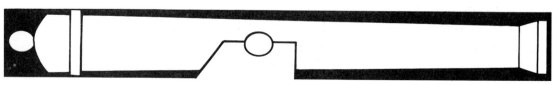

Name _____

The Civil War
(continued)

Directions: *Read the entire passage on page 40. Twelve vocabulary words have been printed in bold type, underlined, and numbered. Look at the corresponding numbers and words on this page. Find and underline the best definition for each word as it is used in the sentence. Mark the correct bubble on the answer sheet.*

1. **secede**
   a. succeed
   b. divide
   c. withdraw
   d. plant

2. **urged**
   a. revolted
   b. strongly encouraged
   c. repeated
   d. reviewed

3. **superior**
   a. better
   b. complete
   c. superstitious
   d. reluctant

4. **expeditiously**
   a. slowly
   b. cautiously
   c. carefully
   d. quickly

5. **fleet**
   a. group
   b. square
   c. house
   d. army

6. **strategy**
   a. hypothesis
   b. precise location
   c. careful plan
   d. mentality

7. **blockade**
   a. banish
   b. built
   c. obstruct
   d. construct

8. **seize**
   a. size up
   b. capture
   c. confront
   d. select

9. **issued**
   a. put forth
   b. canceled
   c. displaced
   d. received

10. **staggering**
    a. stumbling
    b. crawling
    c. overwhelming
    d. staged

11. **immense**
    a. immediate
    b. radical
    c. narrow
    d. enormous

12. **rift**
    a. stand
    b. breach
    c. idea
    d. boundary

number correct _____

percentage _____

Vocabulary Test Prep
© The Learning Works, Inc.

Name _____

The Gold Rush

Directions: *Read the entire passage on this page. Twelve words have been printed in bold type, underlined, and numbered. Look at the corresponding numbers and words on the following page. Find and underline the best definition for each word as it is used in the sentence.*

John Sutter was a Swiss **immigrant** who came to America in 1834. He built a (1)
fort that became a resting place for pioneers coming to northern California. He
hired James Marshall as a carpenter and manager of his sawmill in the
Sacramento Valley, about forty miles away from the fort.

On January 24, 1848, James Marshall noticed shiny **fragments** of glittering (2)
metal at the sawmill. He had found gold!

News of the gold **strike** spread rapidly, and more than 80,000 people from all (3)
walks of life — factory workers, farmers, teachers, and lawyers — **journeyed** (4)
to California to strike it rich. Many **abandoned** their jobs, homes, and families (5)
to travel west. Gold-rush miners were called forty-niners because they began
their journey to search for gold in 1849.

Some **prospectors** came by land traveling in covered wagons. This was a very (6)
perilous journey that took many months. Others from the East sailed around (7)
South America and then headed north up the Pacific Ocean to California. Still
others traveled by ship to Panama, went across Panama by land, and then took
a ship to California.

Not all prospectors struck it rich. But even those who didn't find gold discovered other riches. California was **teeming** with new people and there were (8)
numerous opportunities for farming because of California's **fertile** soil. Some (9)
people **established** businesses that catered to the forty-niners. Clothing stores, (10)
hotels, restaurants, mining equipment stores, and other businesses sprung up.

As a result of the Gold Rush, new cities were founded in California. The
California gold rush **transformed** San Francisco from a **tranquil** outpost to a (11)(12)
major city with many thriving businesses.

Name _____

The Gold Rush
(continued)

Directions: Read the entire passage on page 42. Twelve vocabulary words have been printed in bold type, underlined, and numbered. Look at the corresponding numbers and words on this page. Find and underline the best definition for each word as it is used in the sentence. Mark the correct bubble on the answer sheet.

1. **immigrant: a person who**
   a. comes from one country to live in another country
   b. depends on the land for a living
   c. is employed by the government
   d. lives in a city

2. **fragments**
   a. fractions
   b. land parcels
   c. broken-off pieces
   d. frames

3. **strike**
   a. rebellion
   b. work stoppage
   c. military attack
   d. discovery

4. **journeyed**
   a. traveled
   b. discovered
   c. poked
   d. blew

5. **abandoned**
   a. abated
   b. left
   c. renewed
   d. discharged

6. **prospectors**
   a. government officials
   b. missionaries
   c. reporters
   d. gold-seekers

7. **perilous**
   a. precious
   b. dangerous
   c. primitive
   d. brave

8. **teeming**
   a. pairing up
   b. hanging on
   c. dividing
   d. overflowing

9. **fertile**
   a. rich
   b. ruined
   c. useless
   d. churned

10. **established**
    a. discarded
    b. discounted
    c. set up
    d. closed

11. **transformed**
    a. changed
    b. translated
    c. ordained
    d. transpired

12. **tranquil**
    a. bustling
    b. peaceful; calm
    c. popular
    d. sensible

number correct _____

percentage _____

Vocabulary Test Prep
© The Learning Works, Inc.

Answers for Words in Context Exercises

Pages 28-29 • Archaeology

1. b digging
2. d Unusual
3. d disclose
4. a carefully
5. a exactly
6. d tiny
7. c examination
8. a makeup
9. b distinctive
10. a beliefs
11. d remarkable
12. d seek

Pages 30-31 • The Architecture and Art of Ancient Egypt

1. d location
2. a famous
3. d rate
4. b achievement
5. c sanctuary
6. c important
7. b about
8. c holy
9. a depictions
10. b rebirth
11. d graphic
12. a many

Pages 32-33 • The Aztecs

1. b powerful
2. d prisoners
3. b Before
4. d confer
5. a ornate
6. c decorated
7. c represent
8. a made up
9. d represented
10. b deals
11. c sensible
12. c home

Pages 34-35 • The Lewis and Clark Expedition

1. c acclaimed
2. d obtained
3. a hired
4. b line of travel
5. c profitable
6. b detailed
7. c associations
8. a met
9. d portion
10. b small ornaments or gifts
11. b beginning
12. c strenuous

Pages 36-37 • Life in Colonial America

1. d thrived
2. c diversity
3. c involved
4. a trainees
5. b introduced
6. d plentiful
7. b make
8. a skillful
9. d improve
10. b supplied
11. b different
12. c representative

Pages 38-39 • The Boston Tea Party

1. b permitted
2. d made possible
3. d establish by authority
4. c objected
5. a refusal to have dealings with
6. c threw
7. a angered
8. c revenge
9. b limited
10. d prohibited
11. d approval
12. b assume or accept

Pages 40-41 • The Civil War

1. c withdraw
2. b strongly encouraged
3. a better
4. d quickly
5. a group
6. c careful plan
7. c obstruct
8. b capture
9. a put forth
10. c overwhelming
11. d enormous
12. b breach

Pages 42-43 • The Gold Rush

1. a. comes from one country to live in another country
2. c broken-off pieces
3. d discovery
4. a traveled
5. b left
6. d gold-seekers
7. b dangerous
8. d overflowing
9. a rich
10. c set up
11. a changed
12. b peaceful; calm

Section 3
Words With
Multiple Meanings

Words With Multiple Meanings

This section of *Vocabulary Test Prep* contains exercises dealing with multiple meanings of words. To get you warmed up, let's start by looking at an example using the word **home**.

The word **home** has many different meanings depending how it is used in the context of a sentence. In some cases, it is used as a noun. In other cases, it is used as an adverb. It can even be used as a verb. Here are some examples:

- Our neighbors are building an addition to their **home**.
  In this sentence, **home** is used as a noun meaning "one's place of residence."

- Santa Barbara is **home** to a beautiful Spanish mission founded in 1786.
  In this sentence, **home** is used as a noun meaning "headquarters."

- I have to go **home** to pick up the letter I forgot to mail this morning.
  In this sentence, **home** is used as an adverb meaning "to, from, or at one's home."

- Mom works as a loan officer at the **home** branch of Midwestern Bank and Trust.
  In this sentence, **home** is used as an adjective meaning "a place of origin or base of operations." It modifies the noun *branch*.

- As an experienced actress, she feels right **at home** on the stage.
  In this sentence, the phrase **at home** is used as an adjective meaning "on familiar ground."

- The baby bird will **home** in on its nest after its first flight.
  In this sentence, **home** is used as a verb meaning "to return to one's birthplace by using a landmark."

Make up sentences showing the multiple meanings of the word **camp**. Use the word **camp** as a noun, verb, and adjective in different sentences. Use your dictionary if you need help.

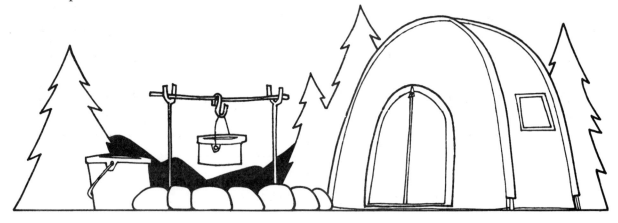

Match a Meaning

*The word **drop** is used in six different ways in the sentences below.*
*Match the use of the word **drop** with its various meanings.*

1. ____ **Drop** what you are doing and come here immediately!
2. ____ I'll **drop** the kids off at soccer practice on my way to work.
3. ____ The vet wants our dog to **drop** a few pounds before her next visit.
4. ____ There is only a **drop** of water left in the canteen
5. ____ The museum curator was careful not to **drop** the priceless vase.
6. ____ If you **drop** the price on your used CDs, they'll sell faster.

multiple meanings of the word "drop"
   a. deposit
   b. lower
   c. small quantity of liquid
   d. lose
   e. cause to fall
   f. discontinue

---

*The word **last** is used in six different ways in the sentences below.*
*Match the use of the word **last** with its various meanings.*

1. ____ The **last** chapter of my book was the most exciting.
2. ____ At **last** he received the award and the honor that he deserved.
3. ____ Everyone hopes this drought will not **last** much longer.
4. ____ She came in **last** in the race, but she was proud of herself for finishing.
5. ____ There is only enough milk to **last** another day.
6. ____ I **last** saw my cousin when we went to Miami for a visit.

multiple meanings of the word "light"
   a. finally
   b. lowest in rank or standing
   c. final
   d. to be enough to meet the needs of
   e. continue
   f. most recently

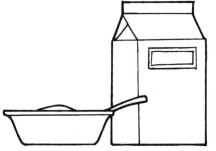

number correct _____   percentage _____

Vocabulary Test Prep
© The Learning Works, Inc.

Name _____

More Match a Meanings

---

*The word **catch** is used in six different ways in the sentences below.
Match the use of the word **catch** with its various meanings.*

---

1. ____ Be careful you don't **catch** your heel on that hose.
2. ____ I hope she doesn't **catch** my cold when she visits us next week.
3. ____ Dad dashed off to **catch** the bus to work.
4. ____ The police hope to **catch** the suspect off guard.
5. ____ There must be a **catch** to solving this puzzle.
6. ____ Let's get everyone together and play **catch** after the barbecue.

multiple meanings of the word "catch"
   a. capture or seize
   b. to become affected by
   c. a complication
   d. to get aboard on time
   e. a game in which a ball is thrown and caught
   f. to get entangled

---

*The word **light** is used in six different ways in the sentences below.
Match the use of the word **light** with its various meanings.*

---

1. ____ He wore a **light** blue shirt with a red tie.
2. ____ Please **light** the barbecue so we can start dinner.
3. ____ The package was **light** and easy to carry.
4. ____ Mom asked me to turn on the **light** in the den.
5. ____ Dad stopped at the red **light**.
6. ____ I was **light** three dollars when it came time to pay the bill.

multiple meanings of the word "light"
   a. ignite
   b. not heavy
   c. short
   d. pale
   e. traffic signal
   f. lamp

number correct _____   percentage _____

Name _____

Exercise #1

Directions: Read the sentence in bold. Notice how the underlined word is used in the sentence. Read the other four sentences. Find the sentence in which the underlined word is used in the same way as the underlined word in the first sentence. For example, if the word is used as a noun in the sample sentence, then the sentence you select as the correct answer must also use the underlined word as a noun. Fill in the correct bubble on the answer sheet.

1. **back**

   The <u>back</u> wall was painted a pale shade of blue.
   a. Dad sprained his <u>back</u> when he moved the couch into the family room.
   b. I hope you will <u>back</u> me when I run for class president.
   c. She stored the paint in the <u>back</u> cabinet so it would be out of the way.
   d. He had to <u>back</u> out of the play when he got the flu.

2. **spring**

   My sister is coming home from college over <u>spring</u> break.
   a. The nursery has a sale on <u>spring</u> flowers.
   b. The cougar drank from the cool water that flowed from the <u>spring</u>.
   c. I saw the deer <u>spring</u> forward through the trees and into the open meadow.
   d. The chair had worn fabric and one <u>spring</u> was poking out.

3. **fine**

   The judge ordered her to pay a hundred-dollar <u>fine</u> for the traffic violation.
   a. There was a <u>fine</u> layer of dust on the furniture.
   b. It is a <u>fine</u> day without a cloud in sight.
   c. His cold is better, and he is feeling <u>fine</u>.
   d. She had a <u>fine</u> on her overdue library book.

4. **place**

   In the first <u>place</u>, you were given incorrect information.
   a. They have a summer <u>place</u> on the lake where they vacation every year.
   b. Steve came in second <u>place</u> in the marathon.
   c. We set a <u>place</u> at the head of the table for our grandmother.
   d. Please <u>place</u> the books on my desk before you leave.

5. **roll**

   I taught our dog how to <u>roll</u> over.
   a. I dropped the <u>roll</u> on the floor when I reached for the butter.
   b. The kids like to <u>roll</u> down the grassy hill.
   c. The store owner deposited a <u>roll</u> of coins in the bank.
   d. During the parade, the drum <u>roll</u> could be heard blocks away.

   ┌───┐

   number correct _____   percentage _____

   └───┘

Vocabulary Test Prep
© The Learning Works, Inc.

Name _____

Exercise #2

Directions: Read the sentence in bold. Notice how the underlined word is used in the sentence. Read the other four sentences. Find the sentence in which the underlined word is used in the same way as the underlined word in the first sentence. For example, if the word is used as a noun in the sample sentence, then the sentence you select as the correct answer must also use the underlined word as a noun. Fill in the correct bubble on the answer sheet.

1. **broke**
   She went <u>broke</u> because she charged too much on her credit cards.
   a. The television talk host <u>broke</u> for a commercial.
   b. Grandma's face <u>broke</u> into a smile when she saw all of us at the front door.
   c. The vase fell to the floor and <u>broke</u> when I accidentally hit it with my elbow.
   d. I was <u>broke</u> after spending all my baby-sitting money on new CDs.

2. **crowd**
   We can all <u>crowd</u> into the elevator if you move over a little.
   a. There wasn't a huge <u>crowd</u> at the swim meet this weekend.
   b. I can't <u>crowd</u> all of these paperback books into one box.
   c. In our <u>crowd</u> of friends, no one smokes.
   d. The <u>crowd</u> began to cheer when the team entered the stadium.

3. **sound**
   The <u>sound</u> of barking dogs woke me up.
   a. I had a <u>sound</u> sleep after all that exercise.
   b. I love to hear the <u>sound</u> of the howling wind.
   c. <u>Sound</u> the alarm immediately; there's a fire in the building!
   d. Buying the new house was a <u>sound</u> investment.

4. **time**
   It is <u>time</u> for us to pack up the car and take off.
   a. Will you <u>time</u> my laps with this stopwatch?
   b. Our class made a <u>time</u> capsule at the beginning of the year.
   c. We stamped our feet and clapped our hands in <u>time</u> to the music.
   d. What <u>time</u> does the party start?

5. **charge**
   I was put in <u>charge</u> of finding a place for our meeting.
   a. I'll have to <u>charge</u> the gift because I don't have enough cash with me.
   b. The tourists saw the rhino <u>charge</u> the van carrying the photographers.
   c. The substitute was in <u>charge</u> when the teacher was called for jury duty.
   d. There was a nominal <u>charge</u> to use the facility.

number correct _____   percentage _____

Name _____

Exercise #3

Directions: Read the sentence in bold. Notice how the underlined word is used in the sentence. Read the other four sentences. Find the sentence in which the underlined word is used in the same way as the underlined word in the first sentence. For example, if the word is used as a noun in the sample sentence, then the sentence you select as the correct answer must also use the underlined word as a noun. Fill in the correct bubble on the answer sheet.

1. **beat**
   To be a good dancer, you have to move to the <u>beat</u> of the music.
   a. You can't <u>beat</u> the prices at this discount store.
   b. The cardiologist listened to the <u>beat</u> of Dad's heart with her stethoscope.
   c. The carpenter <u>beat</u> the nail with the hammer.
   d. She <u>beat</u> all the other entrants in the essay contest.

2. **crown**
   The <u>crown</u> was adorned with diamonds and rubies.
   a. The bird built a nest in the <u>crown</u> of the tree in our backyard.
   b. The <u>crown</u> of your tooth is the part that shows above the gum line.
   c. They are going to <u>crown</u> her "Student of the Year" at the awards assembly.
   d. During the coronation ceremony, the queen wore a sparkling <u>crown</u>.

3. **right**
   The new restaurant is located to the <u>right</u> of the movie theater.
   a. Returning the extra money she gave you is the <u>right</u> thing to do.
   b. I firmly believe that he is the <u>right</u> person for the job.
   c. When you get to the third traffic signal, turn <u>right</u> and go two blocks.
   d. She was not in her <u>right</u> mind when she committed the crime.

4. **throw**
   It's fun to <u>throw</u> a boomerang and watch it sail back.
   a. If you catch the ball, <u>throw</u> it to the person standing on third base.
   b. We are gong to <u>throw</u> a surprise party for Dad on his birthday next week.
   c. The difficult algebra problem didn't <u>throw</u> her during the final exam.
   d. I hope he doesn't <u>throw</u> a fit when he hears the news.

5. **water**
   I drink about eight glasses of <u>water</u> a day to stay healthy and hydrated.
   a. My sister has volunteered to <u>water</u> my plants while I'm away this weekend.
   b. My eyes started to <u>water</u> when I began chopping the strong onion.
   c. Our bodies are made mostly of <u>water</u>.
   d. My younger sister is a <u>water</u> girl for the college basketball team.

number correct _____   percentage _____

Vocabulary Test Prep
© The Learning Works, Inc.

Name _____

Exercise #4

Directions: *Read the sentence in bold. Notice how the underlined word is used in the sentence. Read the other four sentences. Find the sentence in which the underlined word is used in the same way as the underlined word in the first sentence. For example, if the word is used as a noun in the sample sentence, then the sentence you select as the correct answer must also use the underlined word as a noun. Fill in the correct bubble on the answer sheet.*

---

1. **look**

    <u>Look</u> under the bed and see if you can find my other shoe.
    a. The color orange is the latest <u>look</u> in fashion.
    b. I have to <u>look</u> after my brother when he gets home from school.
    c. I didn't like the <u>look</u> on his face.
    d. Did you <u>look</u> for your brother on the school playground?

2. **saw**

    I <u>saw</u> the dog jump up to catch the ball.
    a. The <u>saw</u> is in the garage above the tool bench.
    b. It is hard to <u>saw</u> through this thick wood.
    c. Tell the police officer what you <u>saw</u> on your way home.
    d. The <u>saw</u> was on sale at the hardware store.

3. **act**

    The director of the play asked us to rehearse the first <u>act</u> one more time.
    a. My role starts in the third <u>act</u> of the play.
    b. She is extremely immature and doesn't <u>act</u> her age.
    c. The burglar was caught in the <u>act</u> by the police.
    d. He had to <u>act</u> quickly in order to rescue the child from drowning.

4. **date**

    What is the <u>date</u> of the homecoming football game?
    a. They have a <u>date</u> to meet us for lunch on Sunday at the Century City Mall.
    b. He had to fill out the <u>date</u> of his birth on the driver's license form.
    c. I can't find a single <u>date</u> on this palm tree.
    d. We have to <u>date</u> this antique vase before we can determine its value.

5. **crash**

    The sudden <u>crash</u> of the cymbals could be heard over the other instruments.
    a. She took a <u>crash</u> course in Italian before her trip to Italy.
    b. The automobile <u>crash</u> left both drivers shaken up but unhurt.
    c. The stock market <u>crash</u> affected the life savings of many people.
    d. I heard the <u>crash</u> of thunder seconds after seeing a blinding flash of light.

number correct _____	percentage _____

Exercise #5

Directions: Read the sentence in bold. Notice how the underlined word is used in the sentence. Read the other four sentences. Find the sentence in which the underlined word is used in the same way as the underlined word in the first sentence. For example, if the word is used as a noun in the sample sentence, then the sentence you select as the correct answer must also use the underlined word as a noun. Fill in the correct bubble on the answer sheet.

1. **eye**
   Mom kept a close <u>eye</u> on the baby while he was in the wading pool.
   a. The <u>eye</u> of the needle was too small for the thread.
   b. Please keep a careful <u>eye</u> on your luggage while you wait to board the plane.
   c. The <u>eye</u> of the hurricane passed just a few miles from my house.
   d. The tennis ball barely missed hitting me above my right <u>eye</u>.

2. **game**
   Do you want to join us for a quick <u>game</u> of cards?
   a. We bought a <u>game</u> table at a garage sale.
   b. We need a new <u>game</u> plan for organizing our car wash this weekend.
   c. The photographer was on the lookout for wild <u>game</u> for her photo shoot.
   d. The <u>game</u> of chess requires you to continually plan your strategy.

3. **inside**
   Come <u>inside</u> and help me make some popcorn before we watch the movie.
   a. The newspaper reporter had <u>inside</u> information about the incident.
   b. Her t-shirt was turned <u>inside</u>-out on April Fool's Day.
   c. We had to dash <u>inside</u> when the storm came up unexpectedly.
   d. She kept everything <u>inside</u> and didn't talk about her feelings when her dog died.

4. **long**
   Mom gave me a <u>long</u> list of errands she wanted me to do for her.
   a. She wore <u>long</u> pants to school when the weather turned cold.
   b. Don't stay at the party too <u>long</u>.
   c. I <u>long</u> to see my grandmother who lives so far away.
   d. The football player had to go <u>long</u> to catch the ball.

5. **set**
   Did you <u>set</u> the timer when you put the cookies in the oven to bake?
   a. We had to put sweaters on when the sun <u>set</u> and the temperature plunged.
   b. Gramps is so <u>set</u> in his ways I don't think he will change his mind.
   c. She was given a train <u>set</u> for her birthday.
   d. Have you <u>set</u> a date and time for the family reunion?

number correct _____	percentage _____

Name _____

Exercise #6

Directions: Read the sentence in bold. Notice how the underlined word is used in the sentence. Read the other four sentences. Find the sentence in which the underlined word is used in the same way as the underlined word in the first sentence. For example, if the word is used as a noun in the sample sentence, then the sentence you select as the correct answer must also use the underlined word as a noun. Fill in the correct bubble on the answer sheet.

1. **run**

    She plans to <u>run</u> for city council next year.
    a. The shades <u>run</u> from pale pink to dark red.
    b. I wanted to <u>run</u> for class president.
    c. We saw them <u>run</u> the red light at the intersection.
    d. She went for a quick <u>run</u> before dinner.

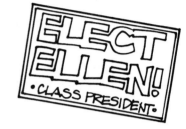

2. **voice**

    I asked to speak to the manager so I could <u>voice</u> my complaint about the service.
    a. She was chosen to sing in the music festival because of her outstanding <u>voice</u>.
    b. Kate is studying <u>voice</u> after school because she wants to become a singer.
    c. Did you <u>voice</u> your concern over the heavy traffic in your neighborhood?
    d. As chairperson, my dad acted as the <u>voice</u> for the people on his committee.

3. **kind**

    She's the <u>kind</u> of person who always takes time to help other people.
    a. She is a <u>kind</u> neighbor and is always bringing us chocolate chip cookies.
    b. Her <u>kind</u> act earned her a medal from the mayor.
    c. Making a donation to charity was a thoughtful and <u>kind</u> thing to do.
    d. The <u>kind</u> of book I enjoy reading most is historical fiction.

4. **quarter**

    My brother's college grades improved tremendously this last <u>quarter</u>.
    a. I found a <u>quarter</u> on the sidewalk.
    b. We are trying to find out why our profits went down during the third <u>quarter</u>.
    c. The recipe said to <u>quarter</u> the oranges first and then cut them into small pieces.
    d. Only the top <u>quarter</u> of the senior class will be able to go on the field trip.

5. **grade**

    The truck lost its brakes coming down the mountain <u>grade</u>.
    a. David's old car had a problem making it up the steep <u>grade</u>.
    b. My sister is going into the seventh <u>grade</u> in the fall.
    c. I ran a low-<u>grade</u> fever for three days when I had the flu last week.
    d. My history teacher stayed up late last night to <u>grade</u> our final exams.

number correct _____   percentage _____

Name _____

Exercise #7

Directions: Read the sentence in bold. Notice how the underlined word is used in the sentence. Read the other four sentences. Find the sentence in which the underlined word is used in the same way as the underlined word in the first sentence. For example, if the word is used as a noun in the sample sentence, then the sentence you select as the correct answer must also use the underlined word as a noun. Fill in the correct bubble on the answer sheet.

1. **pound**
   This recipe in the newspaper calls for a <u>pound</u> of ground turkey.
   a. I finally convinced my folks to let me adopt a dog from the <u>pound</u>.
   b. Michael lost a <u>pound</u> or two after working with his dad to build the shed.
   c. She had to <u>pound</u> nails into the wood when she built the picture frame.
   d. The tutor had to <u>pound</u> the facts into my head before I understood the problem.

2. **safe**
   The wealthy woman put her jewels into her <u>safe</u> before she left for Europe.
   a. I always wear a seat belt when I'm riding in a friend's car so I'm <u>safe</u>.
   b. Although the fire destroyed their home, the family was <u>safe</u> and sound.
   c. It was close, but the umpire declared that the runner was <u>safe</u> at third base.
   d. We looked high and low for the keys to the <u>safe</u>.

3. **move**
   It's up to your team to make the next <u>move</u>.
   a. The doctor told me not to <u>move</u> my arm while she applied the cast.
   b. Neither side wanted to make the first <u>move</u> to end the four-month-old strike.
   c. Let's <u>move</u> this food into the shade so it doesn't spoil in the hot sun.
   d. After being stalled in traffic for fifteen minutes, cars finally started to <u>move</u>.

4. **jam**
   There was such a <u>jam</u> at the clearance sale, we could hardly reach the tables.
   a. The freeway accident caused a massive traffic <u>jam</u>.
   b. He had to <u>jam</u> three large boxes of books on one shelf.
   c. When my aunt came to visit, she taught me how to make peach <u>jam</u>.
   d. Mom had to <u>jam</u> on her brakes when the child dashed into the street.

5. **fat**
   The <u>fat</u> dictionary was heavy and bulky to carry.
   a. An adult needs about thirty grams of <u>fat</u> in his or her diet each day.
   b. The butcher trimmed the excess <u>fat</u> off the two steaks I bought.
   c. She has a <u>fat</u> chance of getting a part in the play because she is always late.
   d. I needed the librarian's help to lift the <u>fat</u> volume of poetry off the shelf.

number correct _____   percentage _____

Vocabulary Test Prep
© The Learning Works, Inc.

Answers for Words With Multiple Meanings

Page 47 • Match a Meaning

1.	f	1.	c
2.	a	2.	a
3.	d	3.	e
4.	c	4.	b
5.	e	5.	d
6.	b	6.	f

Page 48 • More Match a Meanings

1.	f	1.	d
2.	b	2.	a
3.	d	3.	b
4.	a	4.	f
5.	c	5.	e
6.	e	6.	c

Page 49 • Exercise #1

1. c
2. a
3. d
4. b
5. b

Page 50 • Exercise #2

1. d
2. b
3. b
4. d
5. c

Page 51 • Exercise #3

1. b
2. d
3. c
4. a
5. c

Page 52 • Exercise #4

1. d
2. c
3. a
4. b
5. d

Page 53 • Exercise #5

1. b
2. d
3. c
4. a
5. d

Page 54 • Exercise #6

1. b
2. c
3. d
4. b
5. a

Page 55 • Exercise #7

1. b
2. d
3. b
4. a
5. d